This
Calendar
Belongs To

_____

2022

January

Su	Mo	Tu	We	Th	Fr	Sa
26	27	28	29	30	31	1
2	3	4	5	6	7	8
9	10	11	12	13	14	15
16	17	18	19	20	21	22
23	24	25	26	27	28	29
30	31	1	2	3	4	5

February

Su	Mo	Tu	We	Th	Fr	Sa
30	31	1	2	3	4	5
6	7	8	9	10	11	12
13	14	15	16	17	18	19
20	21	22	23	24	25	26
27	28	1	2	3	4	5

March

Su	Mo	Tu	We	Th	Fr	Sa
27	28	1	2	3	4	5
6	7	8	9	10	11	12
13	14	15	16	17	18	19
20	21	22	23	24	25	26
27	28	29	30	31	1	2

April

Su	Mo	Tu	We	Th	Fr	Sa
27	28	29	30	31	1	2
3	4	5	6	7	8	9
10	11	12	13	14	15	16
17	18	19	20	21	22	23
24	25	26	27	28	29	30

May

Su	Mo	Tu	We	Th	Fr	Sa
1	2	3	4	5	6	7
8	9	10	11	12	13	14
15	16	17	18	19	20	21
22	23	24	25	26	27	28
29	30	31	1	2	3	4

June

Su	Mo	Tu	We	Th	Fr	Sa
29	30	31	1	2	3	4
5	6	7	8	9	10	11
12	13	14	15	16	17	18
19	20	21	22	23	24	25
26	27	28	29	30	1	2

July

Su	Mo	Tu	We	Th	Fr	Sa
26	27	28	29	30	1	2
3	4	5	6	7	8	9
10	11	12	13	14	15	16
17	18	19	20	21	22	23
24	25	26	27	28	29	30
31	1	2	3	4	5	6

August

Su	Mo	Tu	We	Th	Fr	Sa
31	1	2	3	4	5	6
7	8	9	10	11	12	13
14	15	16	17	18	19	20
21	22	23	24	25	26	27
28	29	30	31	1	2	3

September

Su	Mo	Tu	We	Th	Fr	Sa
28	29	30	31	1	2	3
4	5	6	7	8	9	10
11	12	13	14	15	16	17
18	19	20	21	22	23	24
25	26	27	28	29	30	1

October

Su	Mo	Tu	We	Th	Fr	Sa
25	26	27	28	29	30	1
2	3	4	5	6	7	8
9	10	11	12	13	14	15
16	17	18	19	20	21	22
23	24	25	26	27	28	29
30	31	1	2	3	4	5

November

Su	Mo	Tu	We	Th	Fr	Sa
30	31	1	2	3	4	5
6	7	8	9	10	11	12
13	14	15	16	17	18	19
20	21	22	23	24	25	26
27	28	29	30	1	2	3

December

Su	Mo	Tu	We	Th	Fr	Sa
27	28	29	30	1	2	3
4	5	6	7	8	9	10
11	12	13	14	15	16	17
18	19	20	21	22	23	24
25	26	27	28	29	30	31

Annual Planner

January	February	March

April	May	June

July	August	September

October	November	December

Goals

_____ ☐

_____ ☐

_____ ☐

_____ ☐

_____ ☐

_____ ☐

Goals For This Year

Key
Objective _____ ⭐

Goal Checklist

_____ ☐
_____ ☐
_____ ☐
_____ ☐
_____ ☐
_____ ☐
_____ ☐
_____ ☐
_____ ☐
_____ ☐

Places to Visit   People to Meet

_____ ☐   _____ ☐
_____ ☐   _____ ☐
_____ ☐   _____ ☐
_____ ☐   _____ ☐
_____ ☐   _____ ☐

Notes

January 2022

Sun	Mon	Tue	Wed	Thu	Fri	Sat
26	27	28	29	30	31	1
2	3	4	5	6	7	8
9	10	11	12	13	14	15
16	17	18	19	20	21	22
23	24	25	26	27	28	29
30	31	1	2	3	4	5

December/January

Week 52

○ 27. MONDAY

PRIORITIES

_____

_____

_____

_____

○ 28. TUESDAY

_____

_____

_____

_____

○ 29. WEDNESDAY

TO DO

_____

_____

_____

_____

○ 30. THURSDAY

_____

_____

_____

_____

_____

_____

○ 31. FRIDAY

_____

_____

_____

_____

_____

○ 1. SATURDAY / 2. SUNDAY

_____

_____

_____

_____

January

01/03/22 - 01/09/22

○ 3. MONDAY

PRIORITIES

○ 4. TUESDAY

○ 5. WEDNESDAY

TO DO

○ 6. THURSDAY

○ 7. FRIDAY

○ 8. SATURDAY / 9. SUNDAY

January
Week 2

○ 10. MONDAY

PRIORITIES

○ 11. TUESDAY

○ 12. WEDNESDAY

TO DO

○ 13. THURSDAY

○ 14. FRIDAY

○ 15. SATURDAY / 16. SUNDAY

January

01/17/22 - 01/23/22

○ 17. MONDAY

PRIORITIES

_____
_____
_____
_____
_____
_____
_____

○ 18. TUESDAY

○ 19. WEDNESDAY

TO DO

_____
_____
_____
_____
_____
_____
_____
_____

○ 20. THURSDAY

○ 21. FRIDAY

_____
_____
_____
_____

○ 22. SATURDAY / 23. SUNDAY

_____
_____
_____

January

Week 4

○ 24. MONDAY

PRIORITIES

○ 25. TUESDAY

○ 26. WEDNESDAY

TO DO

○ 27. THURSDAY

○ 28. FRIDAY

○ 29. SATURDAY / 30. SUNDAY

February 2022

Sun	Mon	Tue	Wed	Thu	Fri	Sat
30	31	1	2	3	4	5
6	7	8	9	10	11	12
13	14	15	16	17	18	19
20	21	22	23	24	25	26
27	28	1	2	3	4	5

January/February

Week 5

○ 31. MONDAY

PRIORITIES

_____

_____

_____

○ 1. TUESDAY

_____

_____

_____

_____

○ 2. WEDNESDAY

TO DO

_____

_____

_____

○ 3. THURSDAY

_____

_____

_____

_____

_____

○ 4. FRIDAY

_____

_____

_____

_____

○ 5. SATURDAY / 6. SUNDAY

_____

_____

_____

_____

February

Week 6

○ 7. MONDAY

PRIORITIES

_____

_____

_____

○ 8. TUESDAY

_____

_____

_____

_____

○ 9. WEDNESDAY

TO DO

_____

_____

○ 10. THURSDAY

_____

_____

_____

_____

_____

○ 11. FRIDAY

_____

_____

_____

_____

○ 12. SATURDAY / 13. SUNDAY

_____

_____

_____

_____

February

Week 7

02/14/22 - 02/20/22

○ 14. MONDAY

PRIORITIES

_____

_____

_____

○ 15. TUESDAY

_____

_____

_____

_____

○ 16. WEDNESDAY

TO DO

_____

_____

○ 17. THURSDAY

_____

_____

_____

_____

○ 18. FRIDAY

_____

_____

_____

_____

○ 19. SATURDAY / 20. SUNDAY

_____

_____

_____

_____

February

Week 8

○ 21. MONDAY

PRIORITIES

○ 22. TUESDAY

○ 23. WEDNESDAY

TO DO

○ 24. THURSDAY

○ 25. FRIDAY

○ 26. SATURDAY / 27. SUNDAY

March 2022

Sun	Mon	Tue	Wed	Thu	Fri	Sat
27	28	1	2	3	4	5
6	7	8	9	10	11	12
13	14	15	16	17	18	19
20	21	22	23	24	25	26
27	28	29	30	31	1	2

February/March

Week 9

○ 28. MONDAY

PRIORITIES

○ 1. TUESDAY

○ 2. WEDNESDAY

TO DO

○ 3. THURSDAY

○ 4. FRIDAY

○ 5. SATURDAY / 6. SUNDAY

March

Week 10

○ 7. MONDAY

PRIORITIES

○ 8. TUESDAY

○ 9. WEDNESDAY

TO DO

○ 10. THURSDAY

○ 11. FRIDAY

○ 12. SATURDAY / 13. SUNDAY

March

03/14/22 - 03/20/22

○ 14. MONDAY

PRIORITIES

_____

_____

_____

○ 15. TUESDAY

_____

_____

_____

_____

○ 16. WEDNESDAY

TO DO

_____

_____

_____

○ 17. THURSDAY

_____

_____

_____

_____

_____

○ 18. FRIDAY

_____

_____

_____

_____

○ 19. SATURDAY / 20. SUNDAY

_____

_____

_____

March

Week 12

○ 21. MONDAY

PRIORITIES

○ 22. TUESDAY

○ 23. WEDNESDAY

TO DO

○ 24. THURSDAY

○ 25. FRIDAY

○ 26. SATURDAY / 27. SUNDAY

April 2022

Sun	Mon	Tue	Wed	Thu	Fri	Sat
27	28	29	30	31	1	2
3	4	5	6	7	8	9
10	11	12	13	14	15	16
17	18	19	20	21	22	23
24	25	26	27	28	29	30

March/April

Week 13

○ 28. MONDAY

PRIORITIES

○ 29. TUESDAY

○ 30. WEDNESDAY

TO DO

○ 31. THURSDAY

○ 1. FRIDAY

○ 2. SATURDAY / 3. SUNDAY

April

04/04/22 - 04/10/22

○ 4. MONDAY

PRIORITIES

_____

_____

_____

○ 5. TUESDAY

_____

_____

_____

_____

○ 6. WEDNESDAY

TO DO

_____

_____

_____

○ 7. THURSDAY

_____

_____

_____

_____

_____

○ 8. FRIDAY

_____

_____

_____

_____

○ 9. SATURDAY / 10. SUNDAY

_____

_____

_____

_____

April
Week 15

○ 11. MONDAY

PRIORITIES

○ 12. TUESDAY

○ 13. WEDNESDAY

TO DO

○ 14. THURSDAY

○ 15. FRIDAY

○ 16. SATURDAY / 17. SUNDAY

April

Week 16

○ 18. MONDAY

PRIORITIES

_____

_____

_____

○ 19. TUESDAY

_____

_____

_____

_____

○ 20. WEDNESDAY

TO DO

_____

_____

_____

○ 21. THURSDAY

_____

_____

_____

_____

_____

_____

○ 22. FRIDAY

_____

_____

_____

○ 23. SATURDAY / 24. SUNDAY

_____

_____

_____

May 2022

Sun	Mon	Tue	Wed	Thu	Fri	Sat
1	2	3	4	5	6	7
8	9	10	11	12	13	14
15	16	17	18	19	20	21
22	23	24	25	26	27	28
29	30	31	1	2	3	4

April/May

04/25/22 - 05/01/22

○ 25. MONDAY

PRIORITIES

_____

_____

_____

_____

○ 26. TUESDAY

_____

_____

_____

_____

○ 27. WEDNESDAY

TO DO

_____

_____

○ 28. THURSDAY

_____

_____

_____

_____

○ 29. FRIDAY

_____

_____

_____

_____

○ 30. SATURDAY / 1. SUNDAY

_____

_____

_____

_____

May

Week 18

○ 2. MONDAY

PRIORITIES

○ 3. TUESDAY

○ 4. WEDNESDAY

TO DO

○ 5. THURSDAY

○ 6. FRIDAY

○ 7. SATURDAY / 8. SUNDAY

May

05/09/22 - 05/15/22

○ 9. MONDAY

PRIORITIES

_____
_____
_____
_____
_____
_____
_____

○ 10. TUESDAY

○ 11. WEDNESDAY

TO DO

_____
_____
_____
_____
_____
_____
_____
_____
_____
_____
_____
_____
_____

○ 12. THURSDAY

○ 13. FRIDAY

○ 14. SATURDAY / 15. SUNDAY

May

Week 20

○ 16. MONDAY

PRIORITIES

_____

_____

_____

○ 17. TUESDAY

_____

_____

_____

_____

○ 18. WEDNESDAY

TO DO

_____

_____

_____

○ 19. THURSDAY

_____

_____

_____

_____

_____

○ 20. FRIDAY

_____

_____

_____

_____

○ 21. SATURDAY / 22. SUNDAY

_____

_____

_____

_____

May

Week 21

○ 23. MONDAY

PRIORITIES

○ 24. TUESDAY

○ 25. WEDNESDAY

TO DO

○ 26. THURSDAY

○ 27. FRIDAY

○ 28. SATURDAY / 29. SUNDAY

June 2022

Sun	Mon	Tue	Wed	Thu	Fri	Sat
29	30	31	1	2	3	4
5	6	7	8	9	10	11
12	13	14	15	16	17	18
19	20	21	22	23	24	25
26	27	28	29	30	1	2

May/June

Week 22

05/30/22 - 06/05/22

○ 30. MONDAY

PRIORITIES

_____
_____
_____

○ 31. TUESDAY

_____
_____
_____
_____

○ 1. WEDNESDAY

TO DO

_____
_____
_____

○ 2. THURSDAY

_____
_____
_____
_____
_____

○ 3. FRIDAY

_____
_____
_____
_____

○ 4. SATURDAY / 5. SUNDAY

_____
_____
_____

June

Week 23

○ 6. MONDAY

PRIORITIES

_____

_____

_____

○ 7. TUESDAY

_____

_____

_____

_____

○ 8. WEDNESDAY

TO DO

_____

_____

_____

○ 9. THURSDAY

_____

_____

_____

_____

_____

○ 10. FRIDAY

_____

_____

_____

_____

○ 11. SATURDAY / 12. SUNDAY

_____

_____

_____

_____

June

Week 24

○ 13. MONDAY

PRIORITIES

_____
_____
_____
_____

○ 14. TUESDAY

_____
_____
_____
_____

○ 15. WEDNESDAY

TO DO

_____
_____

○ 16. THURSDAY

_____
_____
_____
_____
_____

○ 17. FRIDAY

_____
_____
_____

○ 18. SATURDAY / 19. SUNDAY

_____
_____
_____

June

Week 25

○ 20. MONDAY

PRIORITIES

_____
_____
_____
_____

○ 21. TUESDAY

_____
_____
_____
_____

○ 22. WEDNESDAY

TO DO

_____
_____
_____

○ 23. THURSDAY

_____
_____
_____
_____
_____

○ 24. FRIDAY

_____
_____
_____
_____
_____

○ 25. SATURDAY / 26. SUNDAY

_____
_____
_____
_____

July 2022

Sun	Mon	Tue	Wed	Thu	Fri	Sat
26	27	28	29	30	1	2
3	4	5	6	7	8	9
10	11	12	13	14	15	16
17	18	19	20	21	22	23
24	25	26	27	28	29	30
31	1	2	3	4	5	6

June/July

Week 26

○ 27. MONDAY

PRIORITIES

_____
_____
_____

○ 28. TUESDAY

_____
_____
_____
_____

○ 29. WEDNESDAY

TO DO

_____
_____

○ 30. THURSDAY

_____
_____
_____
_____
_____

○ 1. FRIDAY

_____
_____
_____
_____

○ 2. SATURDAY / 3. SUNDAY

_____
_____
_____
_____

July

07/04/22 - 07/10/22

○ 4. MONDAY

PRIORITIES

_____
_____
_____
_____

○ 5. TUESDAY

_____
_____
_____
_____

○ 6. WEDNESDAY

TO DO

_____
_____
_____
_____
_____
_____

○ 7. THURSDAY

_____
_____
_____
_____

○ 8. FRIDAY

_____
_____
_____
_____

○ 9. SATURDAY / 10. SUNDAY

_____
_____
_____

July

Week 28

07/11/22 - 07/17/22

○ 11. MONDAY

PRIORITIES

_____
_____
_____
_____

○ 12. TUESDAY

_____
_____
_____
_____

○ 13. WEDNESDAY

TO DO

_____
_____
_____
_____

○ 14. THURSDAY

_____
_____
_____
_____
_____

○ 15. FRIDAY

_____
_____
_____
_____
_____

○ 16. SATURDAY / 17. SUNDAY

_____
_____
_____
_____

July

07/18/22 - 07/24/22

○ 18. MONDAY

PRIORITIES

_____

_____

○ 19. TUESDAY

_____

_____

_____

_____

○ 20. WEDNESDAY

TO DO

_____

_____

○ 21. THURSDAY

_____

_____

_____

_____

_____

○ 22. FRIDAY

_____

_____

_____

_____

○ 23. SATURDAY / 24. SUNDAY

_____

_____

_____

July
Week 30

○ 25. MONDAY

PRIORITIES

_____
_____
_____

○ 26. TUESDAY

_____
_____
_____
_____

○ 27. WEDNESDAY

TO DO

_____
_____
_____
_____
_____

○ 28. THURSDAY

_____
_____
_____
_____
_____

○ 29. FRIDAY

_____
_____
_____
_____
_____

○ 30. SATURDAY / 31. SUNDAY

_____
_____
_____

August 2022

Sun	Mon	Tue	Wed	Thu	Fri	Sat
31	1	2	3	4	5	6
7	8	9	10	11	12	13
14	15	16	17	18	19	20
21	22	23	24	25	26	27
28	29	30	31	1	2	3

August

Week 31

○ 1. MONDAY

PRIORITIES

_____

_____

○ 2. TUESDAY

_____

_____

_____

_____

○ 3. WEDNESDAY

TO DO

_____

_____

○ 4. THURSDAY

_____

_____

_____

_____

○ 5. FRIDAY

_____

_____

_____

○ 6. SATURDAY / 7. SUNDAY

_____

_____

_____

August

Week 32

○ 8. MONDAY

PRIORITIES

○ 9. TUESDAY

○ 10. WEDNESDAY

TO DO

○ 11. THURSDAY

○ 12. FRIDAY

○ 13. SATURDAY / 14. SUNDAY

August

08/15/22 - 08/21/22

○ 15. MONDAY

PRIORITIES

_____
_____
_____

○ 16. TUESDAY

_____
_____
_____
_____

○ 17. WEDNESDAY

TO DO

_____
_____
_____

○ 18. THURSDAY

_____
_____
_____
_____
_____

○ 19. FRIDAY

_____
_____
_____
_____

○ 20. SATURDAY / 21. SUNDAY

_____
_____
_____
_____

August

Week 34

08/22/22 - 08/28/22

○ 22. MONDAY

PRIORITIES

_____

_____

○ 23. TUESDAY

_____

_____

_____

_____

○ 24. WEDNESDAY

TO DO

_____

_____

○ 25. THURSDAY

_____

_____

_____

_____

_____

○ 26. FRIDAY

_____

_____

_____

○ 27. SATURDAY / 28. SUNDAY

_____

_____

_____

September 2022

Sun	Mon	Tue	Wed	Thu	Fri	Sat
28	29	30	31	1	2	3
4	5	6	7	8	9	10
11	12	13	14	15	16	17
18	19	20	21	22	23	24
25	26	27	28	29	30	1

August/September

Week 35

○ 29. MONDAY

PRIORITIES

○ 30. TUESDAY

○ 31. WEDNESDAY

TO DO

○ 1. THURSDAY

○ 2. FRIDAY

○ 3. SATURDAY / 4. SUNDAY

September

Week 36

○ 5. MONDAY

PRIORITIES

○ 6. TUESDAY

○ 7. WEDNESDAY

TO DO

○ 8. THURSDAY

○ 9. FRIDAY

○ 10. SATURDAY / 11. SUNDAY

September

Week 37

○ 12. MONDAY

PRIORITIES

○ 13. TUESDAY

○ 14. WEDNESDAY

TO DO

○ 15. THURSDAY

○ 16. FRIDAY

○ 17. SATURDAY / 18. SUNDAY

September

Week 38

○ 19. MONDAY

PRIORITIES

_____
_____
_____
_____

○ 20. TUESDAY

_____
_____
_____
_____

○ 21. WEDNESDAY

TO DO

_____
_____
_____

○ 22. THURSDAY

_____
_____
_____
_____
_____

○ 23. FRIDAY

_____
_____
_____
_____

○ 24. SATURDAY / 25. SUNDAY

_____
_____
_____
_____

October 2022

Sun	Mon	Tue	Wed	Thu	Fri	Sat
25	26	27	28	29	30	1
2	3	4	5	6	7	8
9	10	11	12	13	14	15
16	17	18	19	20	21	22
23	24	25	26	27	28	29
30	31	1	2	3	4	5

September/October

Week 39

○ 26. MONDAY

PRIORITIES

○ 27. TUESDAY

○ 28. WEDNESDAY

TO DO

○ 29. THURSDAY

○ 30. FRIDAY

○ 1. SATURDAY / 2. SUNDAY

October

Week 40

○ 3. MONDAY

PRIORITIES

○ 4. TUESDAY

○ 5. WEDNESDAY

TO DO

○ 6. THURSDAY

○ 7. FRIDAY

○ 8. SATURDAY / 9. SUNDAY

October

Week 41

○ 10. MONDAY

PRIORITIES

○ 11. TUESDAY

○ 12. WEDNESDAY

TO DO

○ 13. THURSDAY

○ 14. FRIDAY

○ 15. SATURDAY / 16. SUNDAY

October

○ 17. MONDAY

PRIORITIES

○ 18. TUESDAY

○ 19. WEDNESDAY

TO DO

○ 20. THURSDAY

○ 21. FRIDAY

○ 22. SATURDAY / 23. SUNDAY

October

Week 43

10/24/22 - 10/30/22

○ 24. MONDAY

PRIORITIES

_____

_____

_____

○ 25. TUESDAY

_____

_____

_____

_____

○ 26. WEDNESDAY

TO DO

_____

_____

○ 27. THURSDAY

_____

_____

_____

_____

_____

○ 28. FRIDAY

_____

_____

_____

_____

○ 29. SATURDAY / 30. SUNDAY

_____

_____

_____

_____

November 2022

Sun	Mon	Tue	Wed	Thu	Fri	Sat
30	31	1	2	3	4	5
6	7	8	9	10	11	12
13	14	15	16	17	18	19
20	21	22	23	24	25	26
27	28	29	30	1	2	3

October/November

Week 44

○ 31. MONDAY

PRIORITIES
_____
_____
_____
_____
_____
_____
_____

○ 1. TUESDAY

○ 2. WEDNESDAY

TO DO
_____
_____
_____
_____
_____
_____

○ 3. THURSDAY

_____
_____
_____

○ 4. FRIDAY

_____
_____
_____
_____

○ 5. SATURDAY / 6. SUNDAY

_____
_____
_____

November

Week 45

○ 7. MONDAY

PRIORITIES

_____
_____
_____
_____
_____
_____
_____

○ 8. TUESDAY

○ 9. WEDNESDAY

TO DO

_____
_____
_____
_____
_____
_____

○ 10. THURSDAY

_____
_____
_____
_____
_____

○ 11. FRIDAY

_____
_____
_____
_____

○ 12. SATURDAY / 13. SUNDAY

_____
_____
_____
_____

November

11/14/22 - 11/20/22

○ 14. MONDAY

PRIORITIES

_____
_____
_____

○ 15. TUESDAY

_____
_____
_____
_____
_____

○ 16. WEDNESDAY

TO DO

_____
_____
_____

○ 17. THURSDAY

_____
_____
_____
_____
_____
_____

○ 18. FRIDAY

_____
_____
_____
_____
_____

○ 19. SATURDAY / 20. SUNDAY

_____
_____
_____
_____

November

11/21/22 - 11/27/22

○ 21. MONDAY

PRIORITIES

_____
_____
_____
_____

○ 22. TUESDAY

_____
_____
_____
_____

○ 23. WEDNESDAY

TO DO

_____
_____
_____
_____

○ 24. THURSDAY

_____
_____
_____
_____
_____

○ 25. FRIDAY

_____
_____
_____
_____

○ 26. SATURDAY / 27. SUNDAY

_____
_____
_____
_____

December 2022

Sun	Mon	Tue	Wed	Thu	Fri	Sat
27	28	29	30	1	2	3
4	5	6	7	8	9	10
11	12	13	14	15	16	17
18	19	20	21	22	23	24
25	26	27	28	29	30	31

_____

_____

_____

November/December

○ 28. MONDAY

PRIORITIES

○ 29. TUESDAY

○ 30. WEDNESDAY

TO DO

○ 1. THURSDAY

○ 2. FRIDAY

○ 3. SATURDAY / 4. SUNDAY

December

Week 49

12/05/22 - 12/11/22

○ 5. MONDAY

PRIORITIES

○ 6. TUESDAY

○ 7. WEDNESDAY

TO DO

○ 8. THURSDAY

○ 9. FRIDAY

○ 10. SATURDAY / 11. SUNDAY

December

Week 50

○ 12. MONDAY

PRIORITIES

○ 13. TUESDAY

○ 14. WEDNESDAY

TO DO

○ 15. THURSDAY

○ 16. FRIDAY

○ 17. SATURDAY / 18. SUNDAY

December

12/19/22 - 12/25/22

○ 19. MONDAY

PRIORITIES

○ 20. TUESDAY

○ 21. WEDNESDAY

TO DO

○ 22. THURSDAY

○ 23. FRIDAY

○ 24. SATURDAY / 25. SUNDAY

December

Week 52

○ 26. MONDAY

PRIORITIES

○ 27. TUESDAY

○ 28. WEDNESDAY

TO DO

○ 29. THURSDAY

○ 30. FRIDAY

○ 31. SATURDAY / 1. SUNDAY

Subscription Tracker

Organisation	Date Paid	Amount	Duration	Exp. Date	Method of Renewal	Renewal Date

Subscription Tracker

Organisation	Date Paid	Amount	Duration	Exp. Date	Method of Renewal	Renewal Date

Passwords

Website	
Username	
Password	
Email	
Notes	

Website	
Username	
Password	
Email	
Notes	

Website	
Username	
Password	
Email	
Notes	

Website	
Username	
Password	
Email	
Notes	

Website	
Username	
Password	
Email	
Notes	

Website	
Username	
Password	
Email	
Notes	

Website	
Username	
Password	
Email	
Notes	

Website	
Username	
Password	
Email	
Notes	

Passwords

Website	
Username	
Password	
Email	
Notes	

Website	
Username	
Password	
Email	
Notes	

Website	
Username	
Password	
Email	
Notes	

Website	
Username	
Password	
Email	
Notes	

Website	
Username	
Password	
Email	
Notes	

Website	
Username	
Password	
Email	
Notes	

Website	
Username	
Password	
Email	
Notes	

Website	
Username	
Password	
Email	
Notes	

Passwords

Website	
Username	
Password	
Email	
Notes	

Website	
Username	
Password	
Email	
Notes	

Website	
Username	
Password	
Email	
Notes	

Website	
Username	
Password	
Email	
Notes	

Website	
Username	
Password	
Email	
Notes	

Website	
Username	
Password	
Email	
Notes	

Website	
Username	
Password	
Email	
Notes	

Website	
Username	
Password	
Email	
Notes	

Contacts

Name
_____

Address
_____

City _____ State _____ Zip _____

Phone
_____

Email
_____

_____

Name
_____

Address
_____

City _____ State _____ Zip _____

Phone
_____

Email
_____

_____

Name
_____

Address
_____

City _____ State _____ Zip _____

Phone
_____

Email
_____

_____

Name
_____

Address
_____

City _____ State _____ Zip _____

Phone
_____

Email
_____

_____

Name
_____

Address
_____

City _____ State _____ Zip _____

Phone
_____

Email
_____

_____

Name
_____

Address
_____

City _____ State _____ Zip _____

Phone
_____

Email
_____

_____

Name
_____

Address
_____

City _____ State _____ Zip _____

Phone
_____

Email
_____

_____

Name
_____

Address
_____

City _____ State _____ Zip _____

Phone
_____

Email
_____

_____

Name
_____

Address
_____

City _____ State _____ Zip _____

Phone
_____

Email
_____

_____

Name
_____

Address
_____

City _____ State _____ Zip _____

Phone
_____

Email
_____

_____

Contacts

N a m e

Address

City   State   Zip

Phone

Email

N a m e

Address

City   State   Zip

Phone

Email

N a m e

Address

City   State   Zip

Phone

Email

N a m e

Address

City   State   Zip

Phone

Email

N a m e

Address

City   State   Zip

Phone

Email

N a m e

Address

City   State   Zip

Phone

Email

N a m e

Address

City   State   Zip

Phone

Email

N a m e

Address

City   State   Zip

Phone

Email

N a m e

Address

City   State   Zip

Phone

Email

N a m e

Address

City   State   Zip

Phone

Email

Contacts

Name

Address

City　　　　　State　　　Zip

Phone

Email

Name

Address

City　　　　　State　　　Zip

Phone

Email

Name

Address

City　　　　　State　　　Zip

Phone

Email

Name

Address

City　　　　　State　　　Zip

Phone

Email

Name

Address

City　　　　　State　　　Zip

Phone

Email

Name

Address

City　　　　　State　　　Zip

Phone

Email

Name

Address

City　　　　　State　　　Zip

Phone

Email

Name

Address

City　　　　　State　　　Zip

Phone

Email

Name

Address

City　　　　　State　　　Zip

Phone

Email

Name

Address

City　　　　　State　　　Zip

Phone

Email

Birthday Reminder

JANUARY	FEBRUARY	MARCH

APRIL	MAY	JUNE

JULY	AUGUST	SEPTEMBER

OCTOBER	NOVEMBER	DECEMBER

My Favorite Movies

Title:_____
Actors:_____
_____
Published:_____
Genre:_____
Ranking: ☆ ☆ ☆ ☆ ☆

Title:_____
Actors:_____
_____
Published:_____
Genre:_____
Ranking: ☆ ☆ ☆ ☆ ☆

Title:_____
Actors:_____
_____
Published:_____
Genre:_____
Ranking: ☆ ☆ ☆ ☆ ☆

Title:_____
Actors:_____
_____
Published:_____
Genre:_____
Ranking: ☆ ☆ ☆ ☆ ☆

Title:_____
Actors:_____
_____
Published:_____
Genre:_____
Ranking: ☆ ☆ ☆ ☆ ☆

Title:_____
Actors:_____
_____
Published:_____
Genre:_____
Ranking: ☆ ☆ ☆ ☆ ☆

Title:_____
Actors:_____
_____
Published:_____
Genre:_____
Ranking: ☆ ☆ ☆ ☆ ☆

Title:_____
Actors:_____
_____
Published:_____
Genre:_____
Ranking: ☆ ☆ ☆ ☆ ☆

Title:_____
Actors:_____
_____
Published:_____
Genre:_____
Ranking: ☆ ☆ ☆ ☆ ☆

Title:_____
Actors:_____
_____
Published:_____
Genre:_____
Ranking: ☆ ☆ ☆ ☆ ☆

Title:_____
Actors:_____
_____
Published:_____
Genre:_____
Ranking: ☆ ☆ ☆ ☆ ☆

Title:_____
Actors:_____
_____
Published:_____
Genre:_____
Ranking: ☆ ☆ ☆ ☆ ☆

My Favorite Movies

Title:_____
Actors:_____
_____
_____
Published:_____
Genre:_____
Ranking: ☆ ☆ ☆ ☆ ☆

Title:_____
Actors:_____
_____
_____
Published:_____
Genre:_____
Ranking: ☆ ☆ ☆ ☆ ☆

Title:_____
Actors:_____
_____
_____
Published:_____
Genre:_____
Ranking: ☆ ☆ ☆ ☆ ☆

Title:_____
Actors:_____
_____
_____
Published:_____
Genre:_____
Ranking: ☆ ☆ ☆ ☆ ☆

Title:_____
Actors:_____
_____
_____
Published:_____
Genre:_____
Ranking: ☆ ☆ ☆ ☆ ☆

Title:_____
Actors:_____
_____
_____
Published:_____
Genre:_____
Ranking: ☆ ☆ ☆ ☆ ☆

Title:_____
Actors:_____
_____
_____
Published:_____
Genre:_____
Ranking: ☆ ☆ ☆ ☆ ☆

Title:_____
Actors:_____
_____
_____
Published:_____
Genre:_____
Ranking: ☆ ☆ ☆ ☆ ☆

Title:_____
Actors:_____
_____
_____
Published:_____
Genre:_____
Ranking: ☆ ☆ ☆ ☆ ☆

Title:_____
Actors:_____
_____
_____
Published:_____
Genre:_____
Ranking: ☆ ☆ ☆ ☆ ☆

Title:_____
Actors:_____
_____
_____
Published:_____
Genre:_____
Ranking: ☆ ☆ ☆ ☆ ☆

Title:_____
Actors:_____
_____
_____
Published:_____
Genre:_____
Ranking: ☆ ☆ ☆ ☆ ☆

Podcast List

Podcast	Genre	Rating
		☆☆☆☆☆
		☆☆☆☆☆
		☆☆☆☆☆
		☆☆☆☆☆
		☆☆☆☆☆
		☆☆☆☆☆
		☆☆☆☆☆
		☆☆☆☆☆
		☆☆☆☆☆
		☆☆☆☆☆
		☆☆☆☆☆
		☆☆☆☆☆
		☆☆☆☆☆
		☆☆☆☆☆
		☆☆☆☆☆
		☆☆☆☆☆
		☆☆☆☆☆
		☆☆☆☆☆
		☆☆☆☆☆
		☆☆☆☆☆
		☆☆☆☆☆
		☆☆☆☆☆
		☆☆☆☆☆

Podcast List

Podcast	Genre	Rating
		☆☆☆☆☆
		☆☆☆☆☆
		☆☆☆☆☆
		☆☆☆☆☆
		☆☆☆☆☆
		☆☆☆☆☆
		☆☆☆☆☆
		☆☆☆☆☆
		☆☆☆☆☆
		☆☆☆☆☆
		☆☆☆☆☆
		☆☆☆☆☆
		☆☆☆☆☆
		☆☆☆☆☆
		☆☆☆☆☆
		☆☆☆☆☆
		☆☆☆☆☆
		☆☆☆☆☆
		☆☆☆☆☆
		☆☆☆☆☆
		☆☆☆☆☆
		☆☆☆☆☆
		☆☆☆☆☆
		☆☆☆☆☆
		☆☆☆☆☆

Wishlist

WHAT	PRICE

Gift Ideas For Family and Friends

NAME	IDEA	PRICE

Notes

Notes

Notes

Notes

Notes

Notes

Notes

Notes

Notes

Notes

Doodle Page

Doodle Page

Doodle Page

Doodle Page

Doodle Page

2023

January
Su	Mo	Tu	We	Th	Fr	Sa
1	2	3	4	5	6	7
8	9	10	11	12	13	14
15	16	17	18	19	20	21
22	23	24	25	26	27	28
29	30	31	1	2	3	4

February
Su	Mo	Tu	We	Th	Fr	Sa
29	30	31	1	2	3	4
5	6	7	8	9	10	11
12	13	14	15	16	17	18
19	20	21	22	23	24	25
26	27	28	1	2	3	4

March
Su	Mo	Tu	We	Th	Fr	Sa
26	27	28	1	2	3	4
5	6	7	8	9	10	11
12	13	14	15	16	17	18
19	20	21	22	23	24	25
26	27	28	29	30	31	1

April
Su	Mo	Tu	We	Th	Fr	Sa
26	27	28	29	30	31	1
2	3	4	5	6	7	8
9	10	11	12	13	14	15
16	17	18	19	20	21	22
23	24	25	26	27	28	29
30	1	2	3	4	5	6

May
Su	Mo	Tu	We	Th	Fr	Sa
30	1	2	3	4	5	6
7	8	9	10	11	12	13
14	15	16	17	18	19	20
21	22	23	24	25	26	27
28	29	30	31	1	2	3

June
Su	Mo	Tu	We	Th	Fr	Sa
28	29	30	31	1	2	3
4	5	6	7	8	9	10
11	12	13	14	15	16	17
18	19	20	21	22	23	24
25	26	27	28	29	30	1

July
Su	Mo	Tu	We	Th	Fr	Sa
25	26	27	28	29	30	1
2	3	4	5	6	7	8
9	10	11	12	13	14	15
16	17	18	19	20	21	22
23	24	25	26	27	28	29
30	31	1	2	3	4	5

August
Su	Mo	Tu	We	Th	Fr	Sa
30	31	1	2	3	4	5
6	7	8	9	10	11	12
13	14	15	16	17	18	19
20	21	22	23	24	25	26
27	28	29	30	31	1	2

September
Su	Mo	Tu	We	Th	Fr	Sa
27	28	29	30	31	1	2
3	4	5	6	7	8	9
10	11	12	13	14	15	16
17	18	19	20	21	22	23
24	25	26	27	28	29	30

October
Su	Mo	Tu	We	Th	Fr	Sa
1	2	3	4	5	6	7
8	9	10	11	12	13	14
15	16	17	18	19	20	21
22	23	24	25	26	27	28
29	30	31	1	2	3	4

November
Su	Mo	Tu	We	Th	Fr	Sa
29	30	31	1	2	3	4
5	6	7	8	9	10	11
12	13	14	15	16	17	18
19	20	21	22	23	24	25
26	27	28	29	30	1	2

December
Su	Mo	Tu	We	Th	Fr	Sa
26	27	28	29	30	1	2
3	4	5	6	7	8	9
10	11	12	13	14	15	16
17	18	19	20	21	22	23
24	25	26	27	28	29	30
31	1	2	3	4	5	6